BR BLUE
A PORTRAIT

Stephen Owens

AMBERLEY

By the author of:

BR Blue: A Personal Reflection

BR Blue: The North in Focus

First published 2022

Amberley Publishing
The Hill, Stroud
Gloucestershire, GL5 4EP

www.amberley-books.com

Copyright © Stephen Owens, 2022

The right of Stephen Owens to be identified as
the Author of this work has been asserted in
accordance with the Copyrights, Designs and
Patents Act 1988.

ISBN 978 1 3981 1501 9 (print)
ISBN 978 1 3981 1502 6 (ebook)

British Library Cataloguing in Publication Data.
A catalogue record for this book is available from
the British Library.

Typesetting by SJmagic DESIGN SERVICES, India.
Printed in the UK.

Introduction

I took the photographs included in this book in the late 1970s and early 1980s. The period became known as BR Blue. At the time British Rail wasn't particularly popular with the general public; there was widespread disenchantment.

The railway appeared to be caught up in a world of its own, living in the past rather than making strides toward the future. As with most of the nationalised industries, labour relations were somewhat fraught. They were all underfunded and struggling to function. Inflation was relatively high and fuel prices were constantly rising. The railway invested in electrification and everything else was standardised to minimise costs. Unsurprisingly, stagnation and discontent haunted the network. I say this not to exaggerate the fact, but to illustrate how it was widely perceived.

A contrary opinion may suggest that actually the railway was doing a particularly fine job given the constraints under which it operated. It was fortunate to be blessed with a dedicated workforce and supported by the thousands of people who travelled on the trains. For those of us with fond memories of those days, this is how we would prefer to remember that time. The railway may have appeared untidy and rundown, but this could be forgiven. Although it was far from being efficient, it was trying to do its best; it had once been glorious during the steam era, and surely, one day, it would be again.

Despite efforts to standardise, the uniformity only went so far. There were clear regional difference and although the rolling stock was all decked out in the same livery, the regions still appeared to have an individual character. The various suburban electrified lines were one of the more obvious illustrations of this diversity, another being the involvement and support of local public transport executives. Additionally, some types of loco were only to be seen in certain locations. It was very rare to see a Class 26 outside Scotland or a Class 31 in Scotland, and I can recall the time when a Class 20 would never be seen in Preston and a Peak would be considered exceptionally rare.

I readily concede that I was never particularly good at taking detailed notes; nor was I ever really interested in understanding technical issues. Things such as horsepower and tractive effort, traction motors and dual braking seemed overly complicated and somewhat nebulous if not irrelevant. I simply accepted that some locomotives were more powerful than others and went faster, and this was why some pulled passenger trains and others freight trains. When locos received their TOPS classification and new number, I thought this helped to solve some mysteries – it made more sense than the earlier ad hoc consecutive system.

Apart from my photographs, I have very few other items of railway memorabilia in my possession. Once, I did have a substantial collection of books and magazines, but most of these seem to have evaporated. I'm sure some were recycled, given to a worthy cause or a good home. The passage of time has inexplicable and sometimes unfortunate consequences, and I have been absent abroad for extended periods.

Despite being away, I never completely lost sight of the railway, though there may have been times when my interest waned and I allowed other things to take precedence.

Whenever I did return to the UK, it seemed that things on the railway had changed. Some of these changes were minor: the rebranding and the changes of livery; but other changes were more significant. I felt that the railway was moving away from being the one I had known. I realised that a process had started and that it wasn't going to stop. The railway I'd always identified with was leaving town. I'd turned my back and while I wasn't looking it had taken on a new guise and become something else.

Perhaps remarkably, I do have one old notebook. Quite how it has survived I don't know, but possibly it's because it includes my visit to Barry Dock in September 1973. By this time the scrapyard of rusting old steam locos had become a pilgrimage site. As I recall, the visit was on a sunny Sunday afternoon – actually, I have some pictures taken with an instamatic camera to remind me of the occasion. Fortunately, many of the locos here were rescued: bought by preservation societies, and restored by dedicated enthusiasts. Some of these locos are operating today – bearing in mind their condition when I saw them, this is an astonishing achievement.

The photographs in this book were all taken with Olympus cameras, the majority with an OM 1. I would normally use a standard 50-mm lens. For some shots I used a 135-mm telephoto lens; very occasionally a 28-mm wide angle lens. The images have been scanned from print film negatives. I usually used Kodak C41 colour film, although in 1982 I had a spell experimenting with black and white: Ilford or Kodak. Very occasionally I'd use E6 transparency film. Hopefully, every region and every type of loco is represented. Inevitably, there are more shots taken close to home but plenty taken in places further away. Understandably, I visited more distant parts of the country less often. Nevertheless, there is sufficient coverage and variety in the selection. There are portraits of locos and trains in the landscape. Typically, some locos appear more than once, doing different things in different locations. I've always thought it curious that we'd see some engines frequently and others infrequently or not at all. The order in which the photos are sequenced is a compromise. My original intention was to start in the south of the country and finish in the north. I do finish in Scotland, but get there by a rather circuitous route.

With standardisation becoming ever more apparent, some classes of loco disappeared while others became omnipresent: classes 37 and 47, for example. Class 33 locos had started to appear at Crewe, hauling the passenger trains from Cardiff, and Class 31s had begun to appear in locations not normally associated with the class. It would have been nice had some of the more individual types of loco been around longer; it's a pity some of them couldn't have been reengineered and given a new lease of life in the same way as the Class 73s.

The infrastructure of the country is subject to constant revision. Some things have a limited lifespan and it is essential that they are renewed. The railway is a key component of the infrastructure and therefore it is to be expected that changes will be made. The landscape and the architecture are also continually changing and the rate of change seems to be ever increasing. Because of this, the historical context of the photographs provides additional interest. The paraphernalia of the railway stations is also interesting and illustrative, as are the styles and fashions of the period.

Whether the BR Blue era was better or worse than the one we have today is debatable. On the evidence provided it could be tempting to jump to the wrong conclusion. The photographs only illustrate how it appeared at the time and this may not necessarily be the whole picture. Indeed, the world has changed immeasurably in the last forty years, but there is no going back. Despite this, it is part of the human condition to dream a little, and to reflect happily on what was good about the past.

Class 40 loco No. 40025 *Lusitania* at Liverpool Lime Street. The archetypal station in the archetypal city; a perfect place to start or finish a journey.

Class 40 loco No. 40101 at Wigan Springs Branch MPD.

Class 25 loco No. 25088 at Wigan Springs Branch MPD.

Class 25 loco No. 25149 at Wigan Springs Branch MPD.

Class 25 loco No. 25192 at Wigan Springs Branch MPD.

A Class 86 electric loco hurries through Leyland, hauling a southbound passenger train.

Class 25 locos Nos 25050 and 25296 hauling a passenger train through Preston, most likely a returning summer Saturday-only to and from Blackpool.

A Class 40 loco passing through Preston, hauling a short freight train of tanks. Of additional interest in the picture is the InterCity sleeper on the right.

Class 47 loco No. 47597 hauling a passenger train at Preston. The loco has been fitted with a headlight, which would indicate the photo is one of the later shots in this collection.

Class 81 electric loco No. 81017 hauling a parcels train at Preston on 25 August 1982. The train is on the platform that was used exclusively for mail and parcels.

Class 84 electric loco No. 84002 at Preston. Ten of these were built by General Electric and were introduced in 1960. They were the only electric loco to have oval buffers.

Commemorative-liveried Class 86 electric loco No. 86214 *Sans Pareil* in the southern bay at Preston.

Class 87 electric loco No. 87001 *Royal Scot* hauling a northbound passenger train at Preston. Most of these locos were given names that had previously belonged to steam engines of various classes.

Class 87 electric loco No. 87032 *Kenilworth* hauling a northbound passenger train at Preston.

A Class 25 loco between Pleasington and Cherry Tree, hauling a freight train toward Blackburn.

Class 25 loco No. 25124 between Pleasington and Cherry Tree, hauling a freight train toward Blackburn.

Class 40 loco No. 40115 between Pleasington and Cherry Tree, hauling a freight train toward Blackburn.

Class 40 loco No. 40127 between Pleasington and Cherry Tree, hauling a permanent way train.

A Class 45 Peak loco between Pleasington and Cherry Tree, hauling the Blackpool to Sheffield summer Saturday-only passenger train.

A Class 47 loco between Pleasington and Cherry Tree, hauling a freight train of oil tanks toward Blackburn.

Class 37 loco No. 37121 between Pleasington and Cherry Tree, hauling the Blackpool to Sheffield summer Saturday-only passenger train.

Class 40 loco No. 40122 nears Cherry Tree on a beautiful winter morning, hauling a freight train of oil tanks toward Blackburn.

Class 25 loco No. 25213 nears Cherry Tree, hauling a short train of vans toward Blackburn on 14 September 1982.

Class 25 loco No. 25279 at Cherry Tree, hauling a westbound freight train on an atmospheric morning in September 1982.

Class 40 loco No. 40128 at Cherry Tree, hauling a westbound freight train possibly from Carlisle to Warrington on 19 August 1982.

Class 40 loco No. 40174 at Cherry Tree, hauling a westbound cement train.

Double-headed Class 37 locos with No. 37084 leading at Cherry Tree, hauling the Clitheroe to Mossend cement train.

Class 40 loco No. 40199 at Cherry Tree, hauling a westbound freight train that includes a barrier vehicle and ammonia tanks, presumably empty and destined for Heysham.

Class 47 loco No. 47342 at Cherry Tree passing through a Christmas card scene, hauling a westbound freight train.

Two Class 40 locos, with No. 40138 leading, heading west with only a guards' van in tow.

A Class 25 loco heading west through Cherry Tree station, hauling a permanent way train.

A Class 104 DMU at Cherry Tree on a Colne to Preston service.

Blackburn station as it was in 1982, with a solitary Class 104 DMU on a passenger service. The blue sky does at least give the picture a sunny aspect, although the station appears to be in the process of being dismantled.

A Class 37 loco at Blackburn station hauling an eastbound oil train. The building beyond the station on the right was The Star and Garter pub.

Class 25 locos Nos 25277 and 25138 on the stabling point at Blackburn.

Class 40 loco No. 40020 *Franconia* on the stabling point at Blackburn.

Class 40 loco No. 40064 on the stabling point at Blackburn.

Class 40 loco No. 40138 on the stabling point at Blackburn, accompanied by a Class 25 and a Cravens Class 105 DMU.

Class 40 loco No. 40185 on the stabling point at Blackburn.

Class 40 loco No. 40191 on the stabling point at Blackburn. Interesting paintwork: shades of BR Blue.

Class 40 loco No. 40106 shunting at Blackburn. At this time, the green-liveried celebrity loco was regularly to be seen on special trains and more mundane duties.

Class 25 loco No. 25027 at Manchester Victoria, parked by Victoria East Junction signal box while Class 104 DMU arrives with a passenger service. In the background, far right and just visible, is a Class 504 EMU.

Class 25 loco No. 25212 on pilot duty at Manchester Victoria. The sun is shining, but there is snow on the tracks.

Class 40 loco No. 40196 at Manchester Victoria stabled by Victoria East Junction signal box. Despite a little distortion, the telephoto lens gives the photo impact.

Class 86 electric loco No. 86312 waiting to depart from Manchester Piccadilly with a passenger train.

Class 40 loco No. 40096 at Buxton in August 1982. The locos on the left are No. 40192 and probably No. 40097.

Class 31 loco No. 31166 at Wath MPD. This was taken on the only occasion I visited Wath.

Class 45 Peak loco No. 45134 at Sheffield, having just arrived with a passenger train from the south.

Silver-roofed Stratford Class 47 loco No. 47573 at Sheffield.

Class 31 loco No. 31181 at Lincoln. Although the loco appears to be at the head of a freight train, it was in fact a silent scene: the engine wasn't running.

Class 31 loco No. 31218 at Peterborough.

Class 37 loco No. 37041 running light engine at March.

A Class 37 loco hauling a passenger train at Ely. I think the service will be King's Lynn to London Liverpool Street.

Class 37 loco No. 37089 at London Liverpool Street.

Class 47 loco No. 47003 preparing to depart from London Liverpool Street with a passenger train.

Two Class 45 Peak locos at London St Pancras. On the right is No. 45128 at the head of a passenger train, but unfortunately I've no details regarding the one on the left – only that it is a 45/1 with a red buffer-beam.

Class 40 loco No. 40003 at London King's Cross.

Class 55 Deltic loco No. 55010 *The King's Own Scottish Borderer* departing London King's Cross, hauling a passenger train. There appears to be a sound recordist leaning from the window of the first carriage.

Class 55 Deltic loco No. 55015 *Tulyar* at London King's Cross.

Class 55 Deltic loco No. 55017 *The Durham Light Infantry* at London King's Cross.

Class 83 electric loco No. 83015 at London Euston. Fifteen of these locos were built by English Electric. This one was originally numbered E3100 and was a test locomotive fitted with unique features that set it apart from other members of the class.

Class 50 loco No. 50014 *Warspite* preparing to depart from London Paddington with a passenger train.

Class 33 loco No. 33110 hauling a passenger train at Basingstoke. I'm not sure whether I visited Basingstoke more than once, but it a good place to see inter-regional workings and a variety of loco-hauled trains.

Class 47 loco No. 47081 *Odin* hauling a passenger train at Basingstoke.

Class 50 loco No. 50012 *Benbow* in large logo livery hauling a passenger train at Basingstoke; probably the Exeter to London Waterloo service.

Class 33 loco No. 33008 departing Portsmouth Harbour with a passenger train.

Class 204 DMU No. 1404 approaching Portsmouth Harbour. Unusual location and subject matter for me, and the weather could have been better. However, the photo is unique in this collection and adds to its diversity.

Class 73 electro-diesel No. 73101 at Bournemouth. Until recently these hybrid locos were seldom seen anywhere but on the Southern Region. Happily, some have been reengineered and given a new lease of life.

A Class 31 loco hauling a passenger train near Yeovil. Again, an unusual location for me. I've only been to Yeovil once. I think the photo must have been taken while walking from Yeovil Pen Mill to Yeovil Junction.

Class 33 loco No. 33021 waiting to depart from Exeter with a passenger train to London Waterloo.

Class 45 Peak loco No. 45047 at Exeter, hauling an inter-regional passenger train.

Class 50 loco No. 50025 *Invincible* waiting to depart from Exeter with a passenger train to London Waterloo.

Class 50 loco No. 50038 *Formidable* hauling a passenger train at Exeter.

Class 50 loco No. 50047 *Swiftsure* approaching Exeter Central, hauling a passenger train to London Waterloo.

Class 50 loco No. 50006 *Neptune* hauling a passenger train at Newton Abbot. The MPD can be seen in the background. When I first visited in 1969, Westerns and Warships were the locos in charge and there was often a Class 22 pottering about.

A Class 50 loco hauling a passenger train at Totnes.

Class 45 Peak loco No. 45006 *Honourable Artillery Company* at Totnes, hauling what appears to be a permanent way train.

Class 45 Peak loco No. 45103 preparing to depart from Cardiff, hauling a passenger train.

Class 37 loco No. 37256 hauling a freight train through Cardiff Central.

Class 33 loco No. 33018 approaching Cardiff Central with an inter-regional passenger train.

Class 37 loco No. 37221 trundles through Cardiff Central with a westbound mixed freight.

A Class 37 loco at Cardiff Central hauling a coal train.

Class 37 loco No. 37175 approaching Cardiff from the west, hauling a freight train.

Class 33 loco No. 33023 approaching Cardiff from the west with the empty stock for a passenger train.

Class 03 shunter No. 03144 at Landore MPD, Swansea. This 03 was allocated to Landore for most of its working life.

Class 37 loco No. 37188 at Landore MPD, Swansea.

Class 25 loco approaching Hereford, hauling a Cardiff to Crewe passenger train.

Class 25 loco No. 25042 arriving at Hereford with a Cardiff to Crewe passenger train.

A Class 47 loco departing Hereford, hauling a passenger train.

Class 31 No. 31416 hauling a passenger train at Oxford.

A Class 25 loco hauling a short permanent way train at Banbury.

Class 56 loco No. 56054 passing through Banbury with a southbound merry-go-round coal train.

InterCity HST No. 253047 approaching Banbury from the south, possibly on a crew training exercise.

Class 45 Peak No. 45148 hauling a passenger train at Birmingham New Street.

Class 45 Peak No. 45119 awaiting duty at Birmingham New Street.

Class 86 electric loco No. 86324 on the left and Class 31 loco No. 31322 on the right, after arriving at Birmingham New Street with passenger trains.

Class 24 loco No. 24081 at Crewe Works Open Day on 22 September 1979. At the time this would have been one of the last, if not the last, Class 24 in service.

Class 33 loco No. 33013 at Crewe. The loco was running round the stock of the passenger train it had brought from Cardiff.

Class 33 loco No. 33024 arriving at Crewe with a passenger train after completing its journey from Cardiff.

Green-liveried Class 40 loco No. 40106 hauling the *Ffestiniog Pullman* at Crewe.

Class 40 loco No. 40187 at Crewe Works Open Day on 22 September 1979.

Class 47 loco No. 47089 *Amazon* at Crewe Works on 22 September 1979.

Class 82 electric loco No. 82004 hauling a passenger train at Crewe. Ten of these locos were built by Metropolitan-Vickers, but only eight survived to receive their TOPS number. The first and last were early casualties. I did see the first one: E3055.

Class 86 electric loco No. 86255 *Penrith Beacon* arriving at Crewe from the north, hauling a passenger train.

Class 86 electric loco No. 86260 *Driver Wallace Oakes GC* about to depart from Crewe with a southbound passenger train.

Class 87 electric loco No. 87027 *Wolf of Badenoch* departing Crewe, hauling a southbound passenger train.

Class 20 locos, with No. 20063 leading, pass through Derby hauling a freight train. Part of Derby Works can be seen in the background.

Class 45 Peak loco No. 45121 hauling a passenger train at Derby. The white stripe and splash of red are purely cosmetic, but they do add a bit of style to the loco's appearance.

Class 45 Peak loco No. 45136 at Nottingham.

Class 56 loco No. 56063 at Westhouses. By this time, although there were often many locos stabled at Westhouses, it was no longer a maintenance depot. It was simply a fuelling point with an air of dereliction.

Class 56 loco No. 56087 in large logo livery at Shirebrook MPD.

Class 56 loco No. 56076 at Barrow Hill MPD.

Class 47 loco No. 47308 at Knottingley MPD.

An InterCity HST hurrying south through Thirsk. In this setting the HST does appear to be a visitor from the future.

Two Class 20 locos, with No. 20228 nearest the camera at York MPD. It would appear the front of the loco has received unofficial alterations to the paintwork.

Class 40 loco No. 40197 at York MPD. For many locos this siding was a point of no return; when they were dumped here, they had often been withdrawn. It's not clear if this was the case with No. 40197; it appears fine except for the fact that the horn covers have been fitted horizontal rather than vertical.

A Class 45 or Class 46 Peak about to depart from York with a passenger train on a freezing cold winter afternoon.

Class 47 loco No. 47173 at York, hauling a southbound passenger train.

Class 55 Deltic loco No. 55014 *The Duke of Wellington's Regiment* at York waiting to depart with a southbound passenger train.

Class 55 Deltic loco No. 55009 *Alycidon* at York.

Class 40 loco No. 40064 after arriving at Leeds with a passenger train from Carlisle.

Class 45 Peak loco No. 45010, hauling a passenger train at Leeds.

A Class 141 DMU MetroTrain at Huddersfield.

Class 45 Peak loco No. 45051 preparing to depart from Skipton with the evening Nottingham to Glasgow passenger train.

Class 31 loco No. 31119 on the stabling point at Skipton.

Class 31 loco No. 31207 at Skipton. The old engine shed was on the opposite side of the tracks from here. From this vantage point it should have been possible to see the comings and goings, the turntable, and the locos on the scrap line.

Class 25 loco No. 25150 accelerates away from Settle Junction with a permanent way train.

Class 40 loco No. 40150 climbing away from Settle Junction with a Leeds to Carlisle passenger train.

A Class 31 loco coasts toward Settle Junction in charge of a Carlisle to Leeds passenger train.

Class 45 Peak loco, possibly No. 45025, at Settle Junction hauling a Glasgow to Nottingham passenger train. The service was destined to be replaced by the reduced service featured in the two previous photos.

Dwarfed by the landscape a Class 45 or Class 46 Peak clears Ribblehead Viaduct as it heads toward Blea Moor while hauling a Nottingham to Glasgow passenger train. The desolate scene is dominated by part of Ingleborough in the background.

Class 87 electric locos No. 87023 *Highland Chieftain* and No. 87034 *William Shakespeare* approaching Carlisle hauling a northbound freight train of containers on 7 September 1982. The name *Highland Chieftain* was later transferred to a HST power car.

Class 26 loco No. 26036 between duties at Carlisle on 7 September 1982.

Class 40 loco No. 40069 at Carlisle, waiting to depart with a passenger train to Newcastle on 6 September 1982. This loco was unique and easily recognisable because of the cut-away body.

Class 47 loco No. 47474 in the northern bay at Carlisle. The number is a palindrome.

Class 86 electric loco No. 86249 *County of Merseyside*, hauling a northbound passenger train at Carlisle.

Class 87 electric loco No. 87016 *Sir Francis Drake* with a southbound passenger train at Carlisle.

Class 25 loco No. 25254 arriving at Annan with a Glasgow to Carlisle passenger train on 4 September 1982.

Class 40 loco No. 40133 hauling a southbound freight train through Dumfries on 7 September 1982.

Class 47 loco No. 47570 nears Dumfries with a southbound passenger train on 7 September 1982. I'm almost certain the train is from Stranraer; the branch line on the left is virtually all that is left of the line that once went there.

Class 27 loco No. 27208 nears Dumfries hauling a freight train on 7 September 1982.

Class 37 locos Nos 37170 and 37137 at Motherwell MPD. Initially the Class 37s were introduced to Scotland to haul heavy freight trains. Later, as more were transferred into the region, they took over on passenger trains, displacing the Class 27s and later the Class 26s.

Class 26 loco No. 26027 at Haymarket, hauling a passenger train to Edinburgh.

Class 26 loco No. 26030 at Haymarket, hauling a passenger train to Dundee. This loco was one of the members of the class fitted with double headlights for working the Far North line. The others were Nos 26015, 22, 32, 35, 38, 39, 41, 42, 43, 45, and 46.

Class 47 loco No. 47469 at Haymarket hauling a northbound passenger train. It was unusual to see a Class 47 fitted with mini ploughs.

Class 47 loco No. 47191 at Haymarket hauling a passenger train.

Class 26 loco No. 26041 and an unidentified Class 25 at Haymarket MPD Edinburgh.

Class 27 loco No. 27202 at Haymarket MPD Edinburgh.

Looking hugely imposing despite the weather, Class 55 Deltic loco No. 55010 *The King's Own Scottish Borderer* at Haymarket MPD.

Class 20 loco No. 20175 on pilot duty at Glasgow Central, with a Class 101 DMU in the background.

Class 26 loco No. 26033 arriving at Glasgow Queen Street, hauling a passenger train.

Class 27 loco No. 27002 at Glasgow Queen Street.

Class 27 loco No. 27036 at Glasgow Queen Street.

Class 37 loco No. 37114 enters Glasgow Queen Street with a passenger train, passing loco No. 37051 on the left.

Class 37 loco No. 37051 at Glasgow Queen Street.

Class 40 loco No. 40167 at Glasgow Queen Street.

Class 20 loco No. 20119 at Eastfield MPD Glasgow.

Class 27 loco No. 27010 at Eastfield MPD.

Class 27 loco No. 27107 at Eastfield MPD.

Class 37 loco No. 37027 *Loch Eil* at Fort William at the head of a passenger train. The two locos on the left are Nos 37033 and 37085. By this time the Class 37s had displaced the Class 27s on the West Highland Line.

Class 08 shunter No. 08347 in the north bay at Stirling. When I took the photo this Class 08 was allocated to Eastfield. Apparently, at one time it had been allocated to Fort William as No. D3417.

Class 25 loco No. 25109 at Stirling hauling a Glasgow Queen Street to Dundee passenger train. The loco has no train heating and although there are flowers on the platform, the weather doesn't appear particularly warm.

Class 26 loco No. 26041 at Stirling hauling a Dundee to Glasgow Queen Street passenger train.

Class 27 loco No. 27207 at Stirling hauling a Dundee to Glasgow Queen Street passenger train.

Class 47 loco No. 47197 steaming gently at Stirling at the head of a southbound passenger train.

Class 26 loco No. 26040 waiting to depart from Aberdeen with a passenger train to Inverness.

Class 25 loco No. 25034 at Inverness MPD.

Class 26 loco No. 26043 awaits fuelling at Inverness MPD. The loco appears to have lost part of its horns cover and has had three indicator discs removed.

Class 27 loco No. 27002 at Inverness MPD.

Class 26 loco No. 26038 passing Inverness MPD, hauling a passenger train on the avoiding line.

Class 26 loco No. 26022 reversing into Inverness station with a passenger train from Wick and Thurso. The train will have bypassed the station on the avoiding line because the northern departure platforms would be occupied.

The early morning winter sun finds Class 26 loco No. 26038 preparing to depart from Inverness with a passenger train to Aberdeen. There is something reassuring about seeing the steam seeping from the front of the loco: the carriages should be warm.

Class 26 loco No. 26041 preparing to depart from Inverness with the late afternoon train to Kyle of Lochalsh.

On a frosty morning Class 26 loco No. 26043 is seen arriving at Inverness hauling a passenger train from Kyle of Lochalsh.

Class 26 loco No. 26034 arriving at Dingwall on a serene morning while hauling a passenger train from Inverness to Wick and Thurso.

Class 26 loco No. 26032 at Dingwall, hauling a passenger train from Wick and Thurso to Inverness. The photo contains a collection of minor details that all add up to make the image rather special.

On a sunny summer evening Class 26 loco Nos 26031 and 26022 meet at Achnasheen. I was travelling behind No. 26031 from Kyle of Lochalsh to Inverness, whereas No. 26022 was heading in the opposite direction.

Class 26 loco No. 26036 at Kyle of Lochalsh. The loco has been detached from the train to run around the carriages and take the service back to Inverness.

Class 26 loco No. 26036 at Kyle of Lochalsh reversing on to its passenger train.

Class 26 loco No. 26042 at Kyle of Lochalsh waiting for departure time at the head of a passenger train to Inverness.

Class 26 loco near Portgower hauling the first passenger train of the day from Inverness to Wick and Thurso.

Class 26 loco No. 26035 at Thurso waiting in the rain for departure time at the head of a passenger train to Inverness. Actually, the loco would only go as far as Georgemas Junction, where the train would rendezvous with the one from Wick. The loco that brought the portion from Wick would take the train south to Inverness.